Dreamers
Reality

JENNIFER LAURA HOUGHTON

DREAMERS REALITY

iUniverse books may be ordered through booksellers or by contacting:

iUniverse
1663 Liberty Drive
Bloomington, IN 47403
www.iuniverse.com
1-800-Authors (1-800-288-4677)

ISBN: 978-1-5320-0860-3 (sc)
ISBN: 978-1-5320-0861-0 (e)

Print information available on the last page.

iUniverse rev. date: 09/28/2016

Contents

For

Mother and Father

Dreamers Reality
by Jennifer Laura Houghton

A dedication:

For those who keep dreaming, no matter how big or how small,
Once awake neither you nor any other shall silence a dreamer's call
For those who imagine, and keep the faith, a borderless
world is granted for that which you may create.

But for those who don't, who have forgotten,
Who have left their dreams, let them sit, perish, go rotten,
I pray for you the sand man to be swift, be soon to react,
Never would I wish thee to remain the insomniac.

OCD (Obsessive-Compulsive Disorder) Girl

OCD girl, ocd girl, it's time to come clean,
What goes on in that head of yours, what it means,
Seemingly quirky, but a serious pain,
Let them laugh, but invisible scars still maim.

No amount of scrubbing will make it become clearer,
It's still your face staring back through the mirror.
Psychological web weaving through your brain,
Not their reality, you are quite obviously insane.

Living in your perpendicular world,
Disorder, a train that's jumped its tracks leaving you unfurled.
Anything askew keeps you up at night,
Must be in order to make you feel right.

Wash your hands, but still unclean,
Don't like even numbers, so count to thirteen,
Try not to freak out when something's out of place,
They see what you do, hear what you say,
see the smirk upon their face?

OCD girl, ocd girl, it's time to come clean,
What goes on in that head of yours, what it means,
Seemingly quirky, but a serious pain,
Let them laugh, but invisible scars still maim.

1

Suffer

I'm sorry you suffer, but who says I do?
I wish I could help, who are you talking to?
I'll try to make it better, better for whom?
Trust me; it'll be okay, I'm not the thread awaiting your loom.

Do I seem the disaster ready to crack?
Unwinnable race yet I'm kicking up dust on this track.
Let go, I'm not a flyaway kite,
I will prevail, conquer my own fight.

Tend to the broken, I'm not yours to fix,
Nothing is wrong in this mix.
I'm working on me, one day I'll get it right,
No darkness from shadows in this light.

Start the fire; I'll walk right through the flames,
Tie the ropes tighter, I've already played this game.
A waste to worry, I get by just fine,
Though your stomach yearns, I'm not feeding you a line.

Awaiting my turn to find some resolve,
My mistakes will be mine to dissolve,
I'm not going to worry about your resolution,
I'll figure out how to dilute this mind pollution.

Numb

Tears won again according to the pillow case,
Never would have guessed, by day you must erase,
They don't want to see that, what do you have to gain?
Tears won't solve your problems, or heal your pain.

You'll forget about it, it'll be second nature,
No tears or sadness here, a new human feature,
Laughter and smiles, the only things they want to see,
Don't think about the monster that you will be.

Be the big girl, swallow your sorrow,
Be numb to emotion, though it seems immoral.
Your eyes now a desert, they've finally forgotten,
Smile and nod as you hide the stench of your heart, now
rotten.

The churning, the torture, your soul weeps inside,
You force it down, these feelings you must hide.
Each day it becomes easier, tears don't fall as fast as
before,
Now a lemming, a robot, no warmth to your core.

Years have gone by, and you've become disconnected,
You can't cry when sadness strikes, one tear and you'll be
rejected.
No way to salvage this heart of coal,
Too far gone in the bottomless black hole.

Faceless

Living a life that's not her own,
A broken heart with a broken home,
They all laugh as she cries,
Playing the fool with nowhere to hide.

She just wants to fly over land and water,
But she's suffocating, drowning in a shallow stream,
Still can't feel the ground, what happened to her dream?

They paint her face, smile over the frown,
She acts the puppet, plays the clown.
Daytime comes, she aims to please,
Night falls, back praying on her knees.

Empty

Is that how life left you?
Bitter, torn, and scarred?
Back against the wind,
No hopes of moving forward?

Loss of hopes, dreams, your sacred retreat,
Hallow hole where the heart used to beat.
Sudden changes whisk your dreams away,
Old and new fears keep you afraid.

Now no faith to be restored,
Convinced you're empty and ignored.
The signs have disappeared, which way to go,
Life is drained, do others know?

This is how life's left you, under attack,
Crawling, clawing, to find your way back.
This is how life's left you, youthful years the cost,
Struggling to get through, now just left lost.

Eternity

No hand will be there to wipe away her tears,
Nobody will be waiting for her as she steps off the train,
No one is there to help her face her fears,
Nobody by her side to shelter her from the rain.

No arms to catch her should she happen to fall,
No shoulder to lean on when she's in need of strength.
No voice to answer when she yells out or calls,
Nobody to love, to renew her faith.

Four bodies to lift her limp lifeless body,
A roomful of people to mourn the great loss,
One heart to weep for a love unknown,
One eternity to face the seeds she's sewn.

Always Give and Never Take

Her eyes are tired, but they will not sleep,
Her body is weak, but she will not eat,
Her head is heavy, but a pillow will not feel its weight,
Her body is wearing down, yet will always give and never
take.

Her mirror shows the true reflection,
But she cannot change the mirrors delusions.
Her mind cries for the soul to hear,
But her ears are deaf to how the soul feels.

As they lay her down to rest,
She awakens in her dreams,
Body's last request.

Until I Crack

Push me until I crack,
I won't be getting me back,
When did my star fall,
Crash, burn, never to have it all.

Empty black space overhead,
No words between the lines to be read,
Speak of someone you wanted me to be,
No substance, lack in quality.

A lot closer than I was before,
You laugh and slam the door,
Nothing will ever prove who I've become,
Worthless, every piece I've done.

Can't win what's already been won,
Crawl from beneath the thumb,
Doesn't matter now if you'll ever see,
My thoughts, my words, inner voice, spoken identity.

Just A Picture

It is just a picture, not a memory,
It is not what we are, or what we used to be,
Pictures capture moments, depicts a point in time,
This is just a moment, no rhythm or rhyme.

Poses are flawless, regardless of defiance,
No epic journey, not an inch or a mile,
This picture's worth the screaming silence,
Offered by the emptiness of the smiles.

Dress it up with a frame, it doesn't change its worth,
Fake it all you want, this paper won't bring mirth,
You'll never know the story of what might have been,
Snap another picture, here the truth will not be seen.

Solid Gold to Brass

Solid gold turned to brass,
I thought you were a better friend than that.
I believed in you for years and years,
Never thinking you'd be the cause of tears.

Always giving and taking less,
But for me, false hope and happiness.
You stayed perched on that pedestal,
Ended up just the black hole of a wishing well.

Good intentions effortlessly pass through your lips,
Hurts more not hearing the truth, give up, just abandon
ship.
Who would think you'd ever do wrong,
Blinded fool, walking beside you all along.

Used to be there when I was down,
Seemingly care less now if I frown.
A crumbling pedestal and now I see,
The companion you are incapable to be.

Under Your Bed

Memories left behind under your old bed,
Laughter, clever witty things, everything we did and said.
Forever is a long time, the truth hidden within your core,
You forgot about me when you walked out the door.

New friends took you to different places
where you wanted to be,
Was there ever really a moment when you needed me?
When did you forget all the fun times we had?
Reassuring moments, it'll never be bad.

When did I become the afterthought in the back of your mind?
No longer a friend, never was one of your kind.
What would happen if you stopped to rewind?
Would it trigger that dusty thought you forgot how to find?

As the timeline grows and the past fades away,
You refuse to be reminded of yesterdays.
Believing in only one road,
Why couldn't your story be foretold?

Ringing, nagging, pounding headache,
deconstructing your brain,
Pressure building, thoughts swirling,
never ending, trying to refrain.
Back under your bed where all your secrets used to dwell,
You won't find her there, she gave up on you,
couldn't catch her when she fell.

Only a crumbling trail, too small to put back together,
Blame does not lie with gravity, for it can't
forever hold a fleeting feather.
Where is she, the one you lost long ago?
Not there when you want her, never again to know.

My Goodbye

Don't expect an open window once I close this door,
You're no longer welcome; it'll never be like before.
Once, twice, three times, I let you break my heart,
But not this time, never again, you are no longer allowed in.

Maybe this time will be different; I'll give
you that one more chance,
I used to cry, forget about it, and give
you back that loving glance.
Just give in no matter how many times I fell,
But now I've learned my lesson, learned it well.

This is my goodbye forever, not a see
you later, or write back soon,
Never will I see your face, hear your voice, or
be the sun eclipsed by the moon.
Take back your letters, every song, and every poem you wrote,
Now I can't believe a single phrase, rhyme, or note.

Running free, no looking back, breaking loose, from these chains,
my life, my soul, my heart, are mine, nevermore for you to regain.
I'm moving on, moving forward, with this heart I have to mend,
Not yours for the taking, soul's eye is
watching, waiting, ready to defend.

This is my goodbye forever, time to turn and walk away,
Solid ground beneath my feet, standing firm, no shades of grey.
Tomorrow I'll start to forget, another memory will fade,
Time leave some footprints, new destiny to be made.

What Does Sorry Mean

What does sorry mean when you won't look me in the eye?
Is this it, are we done, is this goodbye?
How strong is your bridge when its structure is lies?
Watch me now as I forget how to cry.

I've given up on you,
Your history contains no truths,
Wouldn't have thought we'd ever be through,
Barely begun, back to one, no longer two.

The heart still skips a beat involuntarily,
Now it's clear, hidden instability.
You said you'd fight for me,
Back to falling for insecurities.

One word, look, breath, that's all that it would take,
Every second of silence another piece of heart breaks.
Our future becomes foggy, all that we would create,
Was it that silly, unreasonable to leave it up to fate?

Tail between the legs, run and hide,
Will they say at least we tried?
It's gone, broken, bucked off this ride
Fought and lost, this time we are denied.

Blind Faith

You put all our love on fates shoulders,
"what's meant to be will be",
Deadly statement, should have predicted,
Our love's fatal destiny.

You promised the universe,
But gave not even Earth's soil to traverse.
What happened to forever, that you'll never let go,
Not part of your two year plan, just the script without
the show.

Looking back, promising 'used to be's',
Now broken lyrics to an unfinished song,
Searching to find me where I never belonged.

Brain fooled by a lying heart,
Too blind to see it torn apart,
Believing in the change, like three times before,
Regurgitated doubts, easier for the hopeful to just ignore.
Willing to sacrifice, give up my world,
While offering your forever to another new girl.

Bread Crumbs

Did you catch her when she fell?
Was it your lucky penny in the wishing well?
Tell me did you find the sun in her eyes?
Please ignore the tears under my disguise.

On a cold cloudy day,
Is she your light, warmth, guiding ray?
Does your blind heart see when she holds your hand?
The strong shoulder when you're too weak to stand?

Did you fall in love while I was counting down the days?
Kept me like a secret, hidden in an endless maze.
She has all the actions, all I have are the words.
She has the lingering melody; all I have is one verse.

I'm just the basket when she's the balloon taking you higher.
Her touch holds the warmth; all I have is the fire,
She sweeps you off your feet, as I grasp the broom,
I just hold the candle as she lights up your room.

You chose her over me,
Is she the one, your meant to be?
Were you talking to her when I was all alone?
For me just a recorded message on your phone.

Did you see what you needed to in her eyes?
Can't you feel your heart feeding you lies?
Did she cry on cue, hold your hand,
Said, "there's never been a better man"...?

There's a girl missing you, sending prayers up above,
Did you forget her name while you fell in love?
Caught between fighting for love and setting it free,
Do I fight or let go, will the bread crumbs lead you to me?

Thirty Seconds

Thirty seconds until her alarm goes off,
Thirty seconds until the routine begins,
Why can't she just stay here, the sloth,
Why is it always the same, much to her chagrin?

Faded memories on a broken road.
Year after year, same old story told,
So many things she could have said and done,
Instead every time she chose to run.

At night alone again, her heart bleeds,
But goes unnoticed while she's lost in her dreams.
She doesn't know how much more her heart can take,
Not knowing the truth, or hearing words that will seal its
fate.

Now back to sleep where she does not dream,
Just silence where love and happiness filled her scenes.
Now she feels the pain which was blocked before,
A heart too heavy, too much to ignore.

Thirty seconds until her alarm goes off,
With tears in her eyes she gets out of bed,
A new day to meet, another one she's got to face.
All those yesterdays it's time to erase.

Broken hearts are so hard to mend,
So she'll start with drying her eyes,
Try to raise them to the blue blue sky.
It is time for this mourning to end.

Take notice of the sun shining, win or lose,
Tonight she'll dream and even hit the snooze.
He'll fade away as her broken heart heals,
Finally love will find her, this time it'll be real.

My Sweet Dream

You'll be my sweet dream tonight,
You're the smiles and the laughter.
Head in the clouds, a runaway kite,
Fate reminds me of happily ever after.

You're the voice I long to hear,
The hand I long to hold,
Restoring faith, subtracting fear,
Dissolves shyness and make me bold.

Reveal the secrets of the silent soul,
Leap of faith to descend to destiny,
Missing puzzle piece to complete the whole,
Out stretched arms ready to catch me.

Mr. Right or Mr. Wrong,
Mr. Too Good to Be True,
The bridge to finish my hearts song,
This blind heart wishes it knew.

Fly Away Free

Listen to me, hear what I say,
These tears I cry will not stay.
Little birdie just fly away free,
One day we'll know if it was meant to be.

You may stumble when you first take flight,
But have faith and believe with all your might.
Soon you'll fly high enough to reach the stars,
Just keep believing in who you are.

Open mind and open heart,
they will get you to where you need to be.
Listen and follow, spread your wings apart,
Maybe one day you'll be sent back to me.

Nobody can clip your wings,
Little birdie needs to learn how to sing.
Once you figure out your hearts song,
You'll find the other birdie with the melody to sing along.

Forget Me Not

They all laugh but you don't know why,
You ponder a tear as one of them cries.
Faces of strangers yet you know them all,
Your mind has suffered a critical fall.

Trapped in this unforgiving shell,
My ears strain to hear the final bell.
Forgotten secrets I will never know,
Brain once sharp now a putrid foe.

It will not stop, will not let go,
Draining fiend continues to grow.
If only I could sleep forevermore,
Nothing left but a rotting core.

Stolen soul silently screams,
Returns to its home for every dream,
Don't make me return to that reality,
I will forgive and relish imminent fatality.

Parasitic Paralysis

Wishing to be free from the parasitic
paralysis offered by your foe,
Rendered you full of mind but how could others know?
You waited, waited, but there was no way out,
Your mind screams, screams, it laughs
as it smothers every shout.

Loose lips can't hold the words you speak,
Vanquished youth, worthless to seek,
Insipid snake slithers, slipping through the cracks,
Making sure to quash hopes of you ever coming back.

Constricting, choking, can't they hear the internal attack?
Loss of fight, what does it matter this strength you now lack?
Willing to give in, will they release you, let you go?
Severed paths, unfocused horizon, which
way to turn, who's to know?

Steals the dreams you fought to keep,
Only escape, this endless sleep,
Nowhere to exit, to run, can't find a flame to burn this cage,
Leave it be, close your eyes, let this be your final dream.

Forgotten Utopia

You tell me to stop dreaming as I close my eyes and sleep,
Where else am I supposed to run, hide the secrets I must
keep?
No clipped wings, free to soar, out of grasp, out of reach,
Voices muffled now, soon to be silent, deaf to the preach.

If here is the only place where I belong,
Let me linger, eyes tightly shut, always right, never wrong.
No hot, no cold, just warm sun upon my face,
No sadness here, no tears to erase.

Blurred lines between reality and this fantastical world,
Dare not shake me to wake up, silently sleeping, the hidden
ocean pearl.
Held captive by doubts, just won't let me be,
Sheltered and concealed because of your insecurities.

Forgotten utopia, paradise of freed dreams,
No more need for escape, hunt for a lost key,
Endless, shadowless world, where one can just be,
Concerns laid to rest; this is where you'll always find me.

Say It

Say what you want to say,
Don't ignore me and turn away,
Say it as it is, exactly what's on your mind,
I can take the words; go deeper than the rind.

Not saying what you're thinking gets us nowhere,
The constant second guessing, believe me that I care.
How do you communicate with an empty stare?
I do my best to understand, just be fair.

Not everything has to be a fight,
Resolve the issue, find the light.
Solid foundation, we can fix the cracks,
Work together, stay on track.

Say what you want to say,
I am not one to turn away,
Say it as it is, we will be alright,
Find the words, work through the plight.

Weight of the World

When did you decide to carry the weight of the world on
your shoulders?
When did you decide that your good wasn't good enough?
When did you decide the world's just getting colder?
When did you decide to just give in when it gets too tough?

Unpredictable future leaves you weary,
The never knowing drags you down,
Pressure, stress, nagging, just leave you teary,
Sparkling smile now an unforgiving frown.

When did you decide that it's just okay?
When did you decide to bow down and fall?
When did you decide that you don't have a say?
When did you decide you were never meant to have it all?

Turn around now and face the truth,
Time to realize you've got nothing to prove,
Forgive the lies of your youth,
Life awaits your next move.

Standing In Your Way

The reflection in the mirror, same story told,
Worthless, never good enough, meek never bold,
Reassurances forgotten, reminders way past due,
When are you going to remember, these images were never
you.

You are more than good enough to me,
How much light is going to make you see?
Darkness lurks only in your mind,
Wake up to what you're leaving behind.

Leave a thumbprint to mark your place,
Define win or lose in this race,
Don't worry about falling behind when you're moving ahead,
Try so hard to keep from being this unravelling thread.

The only one standing in your way is you,
Open your eyes, finally see the truth,
It may not be as you imagined,
Time to redefine life's jumbled misguided pattern.

Lucky Ones

We call them the lucky ones,
The ones we could never be,
Cookie cutter masterpiece,
No grey area or in-between.

No misguided path or fork to fret about,
Mind made up, unfold the map for a perfectly laid out route.
Trials, struggles, challenges and a few bumps along the way,
Secret instruction manuals meant for only those who
choose not to stray.

Keep focusing on those "lucky ones",
But ordinary is easy, let them hog the sun.
Convinced they're better, obsess over where they're going,
Can't shake this weight that you're towing.

Gifted with the wrong kind of smarts, your curse,
Bumping into every obstacle, could it actually be worse?
Watch those "lucky ones" follow suit,
Is it worth it to be the same, just another recruit?

One day those wrong kind of smarts will unlock the light,
You'll rise above; suddenly you'll blink and take flight,
High above those "lucky ones", now very clear,
Always waiting to be found, your story was always here.

Binding Fate

Get so far and then take it away,
What are you doing, so close; you were on your way.
Fight to the top then stroll back down,
Forfeit the game, just hand over the crown.

Ladders just stand; you must do the climb,
They won't hear you when you stand frozen, the mime.
Looking over your shoulder, it's just the past,
Cross over; time to create something that lasts.

It's not always luck; you have what it takes,
You don't need them to give you your break.
Go ahead, take it, it's there for you,
Show yourself what you know you can do.

Leave it to them and the shadow will fall,
Rise from the darkness though they wish you to withdraw.
Lingering, waiting, too much time to hesitate,
Open your eyes, have faith, why bind your unmistakable
fate?

Fall Apart

Did you ever have that feeling that you could do it all?
Motivated, positive, goals in hand, laughing at a possible fall.
Did you ever have that feeling that
others would stop and stare?
Wonder how you are doing it, envy in their
eyes as you carry on without a care.

Things just easily happen, fall right into place,
No need to run, no dreams to chase.
It just all works out, life couldn't be better,
Watch as negativity submits its resignation letter.

Did you ever have that feeling that it
was just all going to fall apart?
Turned down, negative, loss of focus, a failure from the start.
Did you ever have that feeling that you'd
be kicked when you were down?
No hands to help you up, staring, laughing, at the fallen clown.

Air out of your balloon; you start to feel the slow leak,
How do you recover, down, out, and weak?
Patch up the hole with everything you have left,
Fight for you; don't let them steal your last breath.

31

Perfect

Focusing on trying to be perfect,
But only making mistakes.
Ask yourself is this really worth it,
Always the give without the take.

Going nowhere, need to renew,
Forget being idle, standing still,
They don't own you,
Never have, never will.

Strive to get ahead, cover up your tracks,
Let them fall through the cracks.
Trying to break your will, shake your concentration,
Criticism acting as the main distraction.

Tell your story, tell your tale,
Let them anticipate an epic fail,
Who you are and who you'll be,
Be you on purpose, your perfect reality.

Silent One

Silent one, silent one, they will hear the words you seek.
They won't miss the rhythm of your heartbeat.
They won't be blind to the lines written on your soul,
Finish what you started; don't keep yourself from your
goal.

Hushed in the darkness you stumble and fall,
Forgetting how to walk you submit to a crawl,
How did you get here, when did you forget?
Skipping the rewind, jumping to eject.

Patience, patience, focus on that which you must achieve,
Hesitation makes everything slip away, remember, believe,
The willing, the waiting, the not knowing if you are able,
Becoming stuck, feel it adhering, another misfit label.

The light will come if you let it in,
Defeat is waiting with the will to win,
Running in circles will lend no escape,
Why such the motive to be fake?

Silent one, silent one, they will hear the words you seek,
Don't give them a reason to make you repeat,
This is your chance, change your world,
They're listening, they're listening, unveil that which must
be unfurled.

The Real

The meant to be that never was,
The high school Prince turned back into a frog,
The two better off as just friends,
When does the longing end,
When does forever begin?

Stop asking questions and look around,
There he stands to sweep your feet off the ground,
Never mind how long you've waited,
This is the better than anticipated.

A broken bridge may make you turn around,
But together through the stream a new path is found.
You are the truth, you are the real,
The beat of a heart when it has healed.

The kiss under mistletoe and at midnight,
Little candies that simply state 'be mine',
All these things coming true, divine.
Give in, believe, heart and mind in sync, knowing it's right.

Soak in the movie magic moments,
Smile, laugh, forget how to be hesitant.
In this world of clichés and metaphors,
You are the real I prayed for.

The Story of Us

Both led down different paths,
Twisting roads of fate,
Neither knowing which way to turn.
Optimism laughing as both yearn.

Focused on a solitary life,
Giving up on questions of husband or wife.
Hope hides, extinguished like a flame,
Looking for answers; someone else to blame.

Waited for "the one" for so long,
The one to take me as I am.
The bridge to finish this hearts song,
Herd the lion from the lamb.

Two wanderers waiting for the real adventure to start,
Now intertwined together, unimaginable world when they
were apart.
Inconceivable, our destinies would bring us both here today,
Though love leads blindly, the heavens wouldn't have it any
other way.

The Impossibility

You were the impossibility that rode into my life,
Picked up all the pieces, forced apart by all the strife,
Blink twice I might miss the best things yet to come,
Who knew this search could be over, my arms around the one.

Rejuvenate me, set me free,
Show me all that I need,
Give back the words that were stolen, forgot to write down,
Flood me with wisdom and love until my heart drowns.

Forgot how to write the heartache,
No more tears spelling it out in invisible ink,
No more does the head ache with useless hopes and dreams,
Stop, pause, rewind, time to cancel the silent screams.

Here's where dreams come to live,
I have it all and am willing to give,
Courage to stand, to sharpen the knife,
Impossible to possible, the new story of my life.

My Beginning

This end is my beginning,
Lasting chapter in my life.
Now my ears can stop ringing,
Plenty of blood sweat and tears through the strife.

That long winding journey, a landmark now marks its path,
Finally its clear, strong foothold, not the stumbling little calf.
Direct others, a reminder; it's always been there within you,
Only your voice can speak for the silent, the unwritten, the true.

Reality lies here, right at my feet,
Instinctually knowing never to retreat,
Years come and go; now it is right,
Seamlessly tell your tale as day slips into night.

Back to sleep, close your eyes,
Peace emerges, the moon will rise.
Smile, now forever a believer,
Silent whisper, goodnight my dreamers.